ID0599525

Praise for *The Race*

"Once in a great while you'll read something that 'knocks your socks off.' This was one of those times."

—Steve Dragoo, president, Solutions Consulting, Inc.

"Every salesperson in the world should carry a copy of ***The Race*** in their briefcase. In five minutes you can go from feeling low to feeling great!"

—Tom Simonian, founder and CEO of Incentives, Inc. and Array Enterprises, Inc.

"***The Race*** is a great life lesson written and illustrated in an unforgettable way."

—Brian Tracy, bestselling business author

"Many, many people will be inspired by ***The Race***. I had 'goose bumps' reading it."

—Mike Singletary, Hall of Fame linebacker, coach, and motivational speaker

The
RACE

SUCCESS IS A JOURNEY, NOT A FINISH LINE

D.H. (DEE) GROBERG

FOREWORD BY STEDMAN GRAHAM

simple ▶ truths®
small books. BIG IMPACT.

Copyright 2016 © by Dee (D. H.) Groberg
Cover and internal design ©2016 by Sourcebooks, Inc.
Cover design by Krista Joy Johnson
Cover images/illustrations © Paul Lesser/Shutterstock

Sourcebooks, the colophon, and Simple Truths are registered trademarks of Sourcebooks, Inc.

All rights reserved. No part of this book may be reproduced in any form or by any electronic
or mechanical means including information storage and retrieval systems—except in the case of
brief quotations embodied in critical articles or reviews—without permission in writing from its
publisher, Sourcebooks, Inc.

Photo Credits
Front and back cover: Paul Lesser/Shutterstock, kleyman/ThinkStock
Internals: page 1, ma_rish/ThinkStock; page 3, Paul Lesser/Shutterstock, kleyman/ThinkStock;
page 9, AlisaFoytik/ThinkStock; page 10, Le Chernina/Shutterstock; page 23, Julia Henze/
Shutterstock; page 28, Totokumi/Shutterstock.

Published by Simple Truths, an imprint of Sourcebooks, Inc.
P.O. Box 4410, Naperville, Illinois 60567-4410
(630) 961-3900
Fax: (630) 961-2168
www.sourcebooks.com

Originally published in 2004 in the United States of America by Warner Faith by an imprint of
Time Warner Book Group.

Printed and bound in China.
QL 10 9 8 7 6 5 4 3 2 1

DEDICATION

I want to dedicate this poem to someone, but I can't think of who. It could be to my mother, who years ago helped me appreciate poetry—but only to appreciate it, not to write it. It could be to someone I once heard give a talk on a similar idea—but it was so long ago I can't remember who it was, when it was, or where I heard it. It could be to my son, who ran a few races in junior high school, but nothing similar ever happened to him in those few races.

So in the end, I realize that the only person to dedicate this poem to is you! To everyone who has ever fallen, felt discouraged, or has wanted to quit while pursuing any type of goal at all. I dedicate it to those who, at the time, were able to muster the strength to get up and try again. I dedicate it to those who, at the time, were not able to muster the strength to get back up. I dedicate it to everyone because it is everyone's story, not just mine.

In this poem, a young runner gets up after falling, again and again and again. Three times. But three is not the important number. The important number is ONE. Get up one more time than you fall.

I equally dedicate this poem to those who have fallen ten times, a hundred times, a thousand times and have not yet found the strength to get up, to try again. This poem is for you too, because this is every man and woman's story. I admire your courage for getting up in the past, and I admire your determination to get up next time, even if it's the first time for you.

DHGroberg

FOREWORD
by Stedman Graham

When I first read *The Race*, I thought it was a great example of never giving up. This is something people always say about me—you never give up! So for me the story is personal. But I know it relates to a lot of other people who believe in the same thing—perseverance. When I share this poem with audiences at my events, I sometimes see people in tears because they identify so much with the story. They had such a hard time and never gave up, and they can relate to the story personally and professionally. I know that you cannot always be the smartest or the strongest, but if you never give up you can win in the end.

You know, you are not a loser when you fall down. You are only a loser when you don't get back up. People all around the world of all ages can really relate to this story because its message is universal. This story is one that parents want to read to their children, teachers want to read to their students, and I want to read as a thought leader to my audiences.

When I close with my audiences, I always share *The Race* with them—it's the very last thing I do. People are so moved by the story because they connect with it emotionally. Their reactions fit right into the message of identity development. You must keep searching, keep building, and keep trying to find out who you are. You must never stop developing yourself.

I am honored to be a part of introducing this book, because I think everyone needs to hear its message. Adults, students, and young people—they all need this lesson. *The Race* has a lot of personal meaning for me, and on top of that, it's a great story. I am so honored to be able to share its lesson with my audiences, and now, to thousands and thousands of people throughout the world.

The
RACE

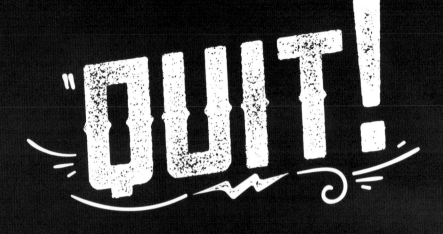

"QUIT!

GIVE UP!

They shout at me and plead.

"THERE'S JUST TOO MUCH AGAINST YOU NOW.

THIS TIME

YOU CAN'T SUCCEED."

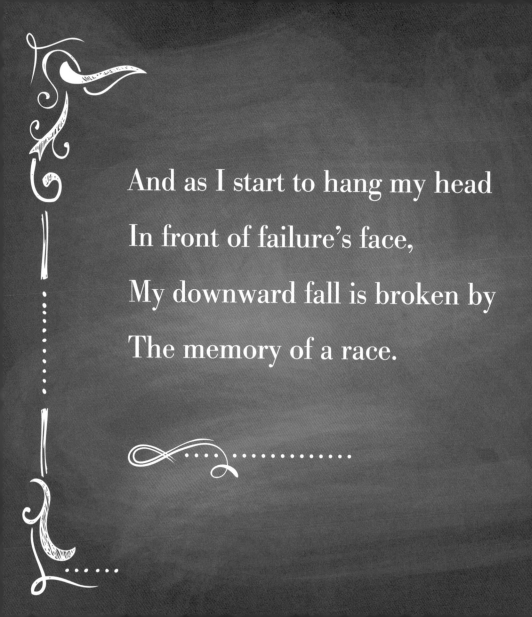

And as I start to hang my head

In front of failure's face,

My downward fall is broken by

The memory of a race.

And hope refills my
weakened will

As I recall that scene;

For just the thought of
that short race

Rejuvenates my being.

· ·

A children's race—
　　young boys, young men—
How I remember well.

· ·

. . . .

EXCITEMENT, *sure!*
  But also fear;

It wasn't hard to tell.

. . . .

They all lined up so full of hope;

Each thought to *win* that race.

Or tie for first, or if not that,

At least take second place.

And fathers watched from off the side

Each *cheering* for his son.

And each boy hoped to show his dad

That he would be the one.

THE WHISTLE BLEW

BLEW

AND OFF THEY WENT

· · · · · · · · · · · · · · · · · ★ · · · · · · · · · · · · · · · · ·

YOUNG HEARTS AND HOPES AFIRE.

TO WIN AND BE THE HERO THERE

WAS EACH YOUNG BOY'S DESIRE.

· · · · · · · · · · · · · · · · · ★ · · · · · · · · · · · · · · · · ·

And one boy in particular,
Whose dad was in the crowd,
Was running near the lead and thought:

"MY DAD WILL BE SO PROUD!"

But as they speeded down the field

Across a shallow dip,

The little boy wh

thought to win

Lost his step and

slipped.

Trying hard to catch himself,
His hands flew out to brace,
And mid the laughter of the crowd
He fell flat on his face.

So down he fell and with him hope,
He couldn't win it now—

EMBARRASSED, SAD, HE ONLY WISHED TO DISAPPEAR SOMEHOW.

But as he fell his dad stood up
And showed his anxious face,
Which to the boy so clearly said,

"GET UP *and win* THE RACE."

He *quickly rose*, no damage done,
Behind a bit, that's all—
And ran with all his mind and *might*
To make up for his fall.

. . . .

So anxious to restore himself,
To catch up and to win—
His mind went faster than his legs;
He slipped and FELL AGAIN!

He wished then he had quit before
With only one disgrace.
"I'm *hopeless* as a runner now;
I SHOULDN'T TRY TO RACE."

But in the laughing crowd he searched
And found his father's face;
That steady look which said again:

"GET UP AND *win* THE RACE."

So up he jumped to *try again*

Ten yards behind the last—

"If I'm to gain those yards,"

he thought,

"I'VE GOT TO MOVE REAL *fast.*"

Exerting everything he had
He regained eight or ten,
But trying so hard to catch the lead

He slipped

and FELL AGAIN!

DEFEAT!

He lied there silently—
A tear dropped from his eye—

"There's no sense running anymore;

Three strikes: **I'M OUT!**

WHY TRY?!"

The will to rise had disappeared;
All hope had fled away;
So far behind, so error prone;
A loser all the way.

"I've lost, so what's the use,"
   he thought,
"I'll live with my disgrace."
But then he thought about his dad
Who soon he'd have to face.

"GET UP," an echo sounded low.
"GET UP AND TAKE YOUR PLACE;
YOU WERE NOT MEANT FOR FAILURE HERE.
GET UP AND *win* THE RACE."

"With borrowed will get up," it said,
"You haven't lost at all.

For *winning* is no more than this:

To RISE
EACH TIME YOU *Fall*

So up he rose to run once more,
And with a new commit
He resolved that *win* or LOSE
AT LEAST HE WOULDN'T QUIT.

So far behind the others now,
The most he'd ever been—
Still he gave it all he had
And ran as though to win.

Three times he'd fallen, stumbling;
Three times he *rose again*;
Too far behind to hope to win
He still ran to the end.

They cheered the winning runner,
As he crossed the line first place.
Head high, and proud, and happy;
No falling, no disgrace.

But when the fallen youngster
Crossed the line last place,
The crowd gave him the
greater *cheer*,
For *finishing* the race.

And even though he came in last
With head bowed low, unproud,
You would have thought he'd
    won the race
To **listen** to the crowd.

And to his dad he sadly said,
"I didn't do too well."

"TO ME, YOU **won**,"

his father said.

"YOU **Rose**
EACH TIME YOU FELL."

And now when things seem
  dark and hard
And difficult to face,
The memory of that little boy
Helps me in *my race*.

For all of life is like that race,
With ups and downs and all.
And all you have to do to win,

They still shout in my face.
But another voice within me says,

"GET UP AND *win* THE RACE!"

CLOSING THOUGHTS
by D.H. (Dee) Groberg

It was the summer of 1974. I had just arrived in Málaga, a beautiful beach resort on the Spanish Riviera. I was a young thirty-four-year-old who had just been assigned to manage training and development for almost all of the international operations worldwide of the then Mobil Oil Corporation. I had invited Mobil Oil training managers from all the company's affiliates around the world to introduce them to my vision and plans for the future. I arrived a day and a half early to assure that everything was set up and prepared for the three-day workshop as I had requested. It was. That left me with a free day.

I knew the Rock of Gibraltar was just a short drive along the coast, so I decided to use my extra time to visit that famous landmark. Arriving at the entrance, I noticed a large sign that said in bold letters: CLOSED. So I drove back to the hotel and decided to use the extra time to finish a poem I had been working on for the past few days. I had heard a talk about a little boy running in a race but falling again and again.

That had given me the germ of the idea, and I thought it would make a nice poem. I just needed a block of several hours of undisturbed time so I could finish it. For a novice poet, it was fun to work on the poem. Ideas just kept flowing until by evening I decided that it was "good enough," and stopped writing. I titled the poem simply, "The Race." I wasn't a professional poet, and the poem certainly wasn't professional, but as I read it over one last time before going to bed, I thought, "This is everyone's story." And with a sense of satisfaction, I put the completed poem aside and went to sleep.

I have never seen the Rock of Gibraltar. Instead, on the day that I might have, I finished a poem which represents "Everyman's experience" in some way or another. As you read it, I hope you will find yourself as that "fallen youngster," and through him learn what I believe is one of life's greatest lessons. The poem is simply an attempt, when everything seems to be going against you, when your failure seems imminent, to encourage hope over despair. Read it. Learn from it. Share it.

When you feel like giving up,
who do you turn to and why?

_____

_____

_____

_____

_____

_____

_____

When I "fell" trying to *achieve* my own dreams, I picked myself back up with the help of...

_____

_____

_____

_____

_____

_____

_____

My most *triumphant* race was...

_____

_____

_____

_____

_____

_____

_____

_____

Perseverance

is not a long race;

it is *many short races*

one after the other.

Walter Elliot

ABOUT THE AUTHOR

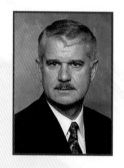

Dr. D. H. (Dee) Groberg is a retired business consultant/trainer whose career has focused almost entirely on teaching and motivating people. He is currently residing primarily in Cambodia as the head of the Cambodian Children's Humanitarian Education Project, an entity he created in order to give more Cambodian children an opportunity to get at least a basic education.

His method of doing this is to identify Cambodian children of school age who are unable to attend school but would like to get an education. Then Dee examines the barriers and takes the action needed to remove them. His wish is that many of these students will go on to become leaders in their own country.

With an education in Asian Studies (BA), Applied Linguistics (MA), Organizational Behavior, and Instructional Design, prior to retirement,

Dee taught leadership and effectiveness workshops to senior executive teams in many countries throughout the world.

During his career he has also learned the languages of the places he has traveled to and worked in—some fluently and others to various degrees of proficiency. He also established an innovative language school in Japan, which went on to become one of the largest in the country.

In summary, Dee could be described as one who loves to be continuously learning, reading regularly on a variety of topics, learning foreign languages, traveling, and interacting with people of various backgrounds from around the world.

In addition to the *The Race*, Dee has written many other poems and books on topics from innovative language learning to the analysis of factors that produce highly effective training.

CHANGE STARTS WITH **SOMETHING SIMPLE.**

Pick from hundreds of titles at:
SimpleTruths.com

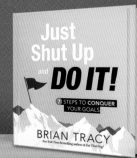

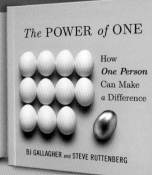

▷ Shop for books on themes like: teamwork, success, leadership, customer service, motivation, and more.

Call us toll-free at **1-800-900-3427**

VISIT: simpletruthsmovies.com to access our FREE library of inspirational videos